Reshaped

ONE MAN'S UNCOMMON JOURNEY INTO
LEADERSHIP THAT BEGAN WITH LOSS AND ABUSE

A PATHWAY TO RECOVERY

THOMAS J. GRIFFIN

ISBN 978-1-63961-777-7 (paperback)
ISBN 978-1-63961-778-4 (digital)

Christian Faith Publishing, Inc.
832 Park Avenue
Meadville, PA 16335
www.christianfaithpublishing.com

Printed in the United States of America

INTRODUCTION

As a young boy growing up in the 1960s and 1970s in Somerville, Massachusetts, I had no clue what I wanted to do for "work" after schooling ended. I had zero interest in going to college at that time, so it was work that I would need to find by the time graduation from high school had arrived. Family members and teachers would ask often throughout those years—actually, *harass* would be the better word—"What do you want to 'do' when you grow up?"

As an adolescent, I gave some thought to that question for a very long time, and by the time high school had concluded, I felt the better question would have been "What do you want to 'be' when you grow up?" My response to that question would have been on my lips more readily. I knew I wanted to "be" someone at the service of others in society. I didn't want to merely "do" something for several decades then retire from the doing. I wanted much more than just another job.

By the time I managed to survive and graduate from high school, I knew I wanted to be a leader somewhere in an organization that served society, where I might be looked upon to lead others through challenging and chaotic times. It was a vague yet, at the same time, a very complex view of service to others and a lofty goal for someone with just a high school diploma at that time.

I have continued to maintain that mindset about "work and service to others" these many years in ministerial leadership, and it has served me quite well, and more importantly, it has served others well, I believe too!

I had no clue at that time what skills would be required of me to lead others, or to guide an organization, or even what type of an organization I could possibly lead. I knew I did not want to merely

3

follow: I wanted to be the decision-maker and the one in charge of my own destiny.

That desire to lead rather than follow others finds its roots in the middle of the universal church's clergy sexual abuse scandal that shook the church and the secular worlds from the late 1990s to the early 2000s, with its residual effects felt still today by too many individuals.

I didn't know it at the time of the sexual assaults I experienced that I would become just another abuse statistic some thirty-plus years later. There's been no acknowledgment of the attack by the religious-order priests who served my childhood parish. I've had a few listening sessions with pastoral support staff and a very supportive face-to-face encounter with the cardinal archbishop of the diocese where I currently serve in ministry. I have not received, nor am I seeking, any type of financial settlement. Like many survivors, we have received lip service too often—mere words that lack real action on behalf of survivors in my estimation.

I didn't know it at the time of the assaults that I had a calling to serve the church. Why would someone who experienced abuse seek a role in this church? Why would a survivor continue to have a relationship with a church that has had such an egregious record of fixing the multifaceted problem? What has motivated me to remain a practicing Catholic when there are other options available to me?

These and other questions have haunted me at times and empowered me at other times as well, to remain in a relationship with Christ through the sacraments of the Catholic Church that I cannot find elsewhere in my theological understanding of being in a personal relationship with Jesus Christ.

People have challenged me often because of my choice to have a lengthy lay ecclesial ministerial career in the Catholic Church and my defense of the church as well: the sins of a few (far too many) shouldn't taint the entire church and its organization. We'll never be able to convict and punish the popes, cardinals, archbishops, bishops, priests, religious, etc. who knew of these heinous acts remained silent or did nothing at all to address the crimes. There are no reparations for this sordid history of events.

What I opted to do at some point early in my vocation of service to church and others was to remain faithful to growing my faith, and to be certain that abuse on a micro level in the parishes where I served, that abuse of any kind would be rooted out, no longer tolerated regardless of the pushback from a priest, bishop, archbishop, or cardinal.

If ministers, lay and ordained, handled the micro, the larger issues of abuse on the macro level could be addressed as well by bold church leaders working closely with victims, law enforcement, dioceses, etc. To date, I feel, the number of new cases—still abhorrent behavior—has dropped dramatically because of the safeguards finally in place. But sadly, these are not enough!

I've been "reshaped" constantly and in a variety of ways throughout my life, through profound encounters, good and bad. Family is that first place of being formed or shaped in this world. Eventually, we grow away from the conformity of family expectations to reshape our identity, and it occurs again and again if you are smart enough to embrace it.

CHAPTER 1

What Is Leadership?

I was not a religious child by any stretch of the imagination, but I did attend Mass on a regular basis and CCD classes to eventually celebrate the sacrament of confirmation in the eighth grade—just a few years removed from the assaults. Once confirmation was over with, I took a break from Mass for several years. Eventually, though, I was intrigued by the church and God and all the bigger questions of life.

I was not quite certain how to pursue a life of faith or deepen my own faith practices. I knew there was more to life than what science could explain. There was a mystique about the universe and its movements that I wanted to further explore and discover every dimension of its vastness.

The idea of someday leading others to deepen their own faith during difficult, chaotic, stormy, and challenging times, as well as times filled with great hope and joy, had not even entered my mind at this point. I was still a young boy who wanted to come home from school and play whatever seasonal sport was being played at that time. I just wanted to be with friends from the neighborhood. I never envisioned as a child that I would have a career in local Catholic parish leadership lasting thirty-five-plus years serving in several parishes in a variety of pastoral, educational, and other leadership roles.

At an early age, I was intrigued by the men and women, those priests and nuns who served at the local parish school and church. They were visible in the neighborhood and roamed the streets talking to the children and adults. They went to dinners at the homes of my friends. They shot baskets in the local park with kids. They played jumped rope with the girls. They played tag. They were very cool to me.

Their visibility and their appearance of being "cool" for all to see might have been that initial witness and vocational tug that others feel when called to serve the church, others, and God. There was a mystique about them in their places of ministry: the neighborhood and the parish.

I knew some neighborhood boys who got along quite well with the priests. They were recruited to become altar boys; the church only allowed boys to serve back in the mid-1960s. This lasted until the early eighties in many places. I, too, wanted to serve the church initially as an altar boy.

My homelife was a bit dysfunctional for a variety of factors. My father died when I was just two years old, leaving behind two older siblings for a mother to raise. His death probably created the dysfunction, or at the very least added to it. How could any single parent, a mother, do all the emotional, spiritual, financial, and physical work needed to raise children? I've never fully blamed her for the dysfunction. It was dumped onto her lap unfairly.

Although we were dirt-poor, we did not know it at the time. We were young, we had friends, we had food and shelter, we had holidays, and we had a small number of extended family members we would visit occasionally. We survived the dysfunction—or we simply adapted to the situation and learned to make it work for us. It did not cripple us, nor did it paralyze us. Each of the three children grew apart over time, but all three were successful in their careers. What did not kill us made us stronger as individuals.

Even at a young age, I saw a unique type of leadership in my home. There was a job to do, and everyone had a part to play. Some went to work to put food on the table and pay the bills while others did tasks and chores around the house to keep it functioning. Some cooked and cleaned, others did the laundry. It was an unspoken team effort to make the best of a difficult situation.

That is the first model of leadership within the context of a family unit where I witnessed people who tried to serve the needs of the others in the organization—in this case, the family. From dysfunction and chaos came elements of survival for the family unit as it was then constituted.

None of the three surviving family members today, the children, would ever define us a unified entity, then or now, but there was an unspoken model of leadership, collaboration, and survival skills that were taught and modeled on many levels.

The yearning to serve the church was a surprise to me as I reflect back upon it now. I cannot explain the emotions of the time, but I knew the church was a place where I felt at home, comfortable with myself, and at ease—until I was no longer at ease.

That feeling of belonging is what eventually led me, with multiple wrong turns and detours along the way, to pursue a vocation, a ministerial career serving others, the church, and God. The church was a place where local, national, and universal leadership was evident to me through her far-reaching power and omnipresence.

The primary motivation for writing this book comes as a response to what I have seen as a lack of much-needed leadership and accountability today—at times but not always—that has eroded the once-strong footing of Catholic parishes as well as the larger universal church in the modern world.

We must also look at the lack of sound political leadership, nationally and locally, on both sides of the political landscape as the nation's values are eroding daily. Leadership in times of crisis and chaos is needed more than ever from elected officials, business leaders, church leaders, and from others who call themselves leaders.

Once-proud institutions, far beyond the church world, have been shell-shocked by sexual abuse claims, financial and political scandals, and poor decisions made by those in leadership at the local, national, and international levels. The church herself and other organizations need new paradigms of leadership if they or we are going to survive these often-chaotic and dark times. There is a duty to prosper in serving others; it is what those flawed framers of our society first envisioned for all humanity.

The church has done, and continues to do, far many more great things than evil things. The churches as a whole (beyond Catholicism) fill the enormous gaps left behind when government agencies fail to provide the basic necessities for individuals in need.

Faith-based organizations continue to remain, collectively, the largest social service providers in the world serving the poorest of the poor; serving individuals, children, and families; being the voice for the silenced and the oppressed, the imprisoned, the immigrant, those living in the shadows of society; and doing those things that no government agency, at this time, seems willing or capable of doing: getting their hands dirty caring for the disenfranchised. Religious organizations lead in so many positive ways yet lack leadership at other critical times—always the double-edged sword.

I have had the good fortune of working side by side with some amazing laypeople, clergy, and religious brothers and sisters whom I still consider friends. We are and were collaborators and colleagues in good and bad times and always tried to provide people with a sense of hope and joy in times of loss and despair. Their examples of partnership is how ministry should be defined—a partnership and collaboration with each person having unique and distinct roles that do not usurp others in leadership.

I have also worked with some individuals—lay and the ordained—who saw their role as the only role and the only voice that mattered in all decision-making. Ministry in today's parishes requires a high level of collegiality and a partnership that serves all, not just the one who might call himself pastor. The people of God are not here to serve your needs!

While clericalism, on the surface, attempts to suppress collegiality today, some members of the clergy are more than willing to share—not surrender—the leadership of the local faith community. In parts of the country today, laymen and laywomen with appropriate skill sets, formation, and education lead parishes in a variety of much-needed new ways. There has been a paradigm shift that must spread as the number of ordained men declines year after year. We need fresh eyes to transform the church today.

This attempt to write about leadership is also rooted in my own experiences of ministering to the people of God in my long ministerial career. I have been at the service of the people and the church during some very celebratory times as well as some very challenging times for the local faith communities, the national church, and the global faith community.

No church, no parish, no individual is all good or all bad. We are complicated people, organizations, and systems attempting to do our best at all times. Yet in times of crisis, we are called to go beyond just attempting to do our best. We are called to be our best when individuals are suffering, when organizations are hurting, and when societies are being pulled apart by internal and external forces that we once relied upon for direction.

A secondary factor for writing about my various experiences is perhaps for my own emotional reasons. Having lived through a sexual assault has never defined me. The abuse did not send me into emotional upheaval, suicidal thoughts, deep depression, or drug and alcohol abuse, as is often the case. I chose food as the numbing agent perhaps to mask whatever pain was deep within—I'll address Fat Tom later.

The abuse did not affect my interest in girls—women later—as intimate partners. It affected my relationship at home as I was never believed and then was forced to deeply bury the experience until the scandal became national and international news by 2000. Then and only then did the anguish of the past surface for the first time. I eventually came forward to share my story with church officials, colleagues, close friends, and others.

It is my hope and my intention as well that by re-examining these past events, the ministerial career path I've experienced, and my willingness to not give up on an organization such as the church because of one or two bad experiences for me might be beneficial for others to hear.

What I experienced could never equal the torment others had to endure. Others have sought financial compensation—as if there is a dollar amount that might help ease the pain. Some have been lost and cast aside by the church and within other organizations where the abuse took place. And still others have committed suicide as the profound pain was simply too much to carry. Their cross was too heavy to carry alone.

This book would not have been written without possessing a deep and abiding love for the entity of the Catholic parish as the true representation of the universal Catholic Church in the world. "All politics is local" as was said by former speaker of the House of Representatives Tip O'Neil. The church on the local level is that representation of the church in the modern world where people live out their lives of faith serving God and others.

In addition, I have had friends, college professors, clergy, parishioners, and some lay colleagues who have encouraged me throughout the years to speak out and to write about church issues, as if I have any real unique take on church life.

To have endured in any type of work for thirty-five-plus years gives me now enough humble motivation to get over the hurdle of putting some words to paper. As I soon conclude a professional ministerial role in parishes, I'm feeling more freedom to speak about my vocational calling, my positive and negative experiences, and my suggestions for the church that I continue to love.

I've never been told *not* to speak out but felt a loyalty to a church that needs her people to be simultaneously both supportive and critical, offering recommendations to grow the church each day in new ways. We can be reshaped, and we can be better individually and collectively than we were yesterday.

I've never dedicated the time nor did I have the desire initially to address my experiences in the church. I never felt my thoughts and ministerial experiences were worthy enough to be considered for publication. I'm assuming here that other writers have used these excuses and others as well when considering an attempt at publishing.

As ministerial work fades into the sunset and retirement approaches, this effort is more than just a cathartic attempt to heal from past wounds. This effort is, like all ministry, a one-on-one encounter with the person reading this right now at this very moment. We minister to one person at a time, as Pope Francis suggested that we treat the wounds in front of us at any given time. This effort is for you and the wounds you've encountered in the church.

My childhood, adolescence, young adulthood, my now-senior-adulthood status, and all the rich experiences and people I have encountered in life and in ministry—all have reshaped me from being that child who lacked a purpose and vision for many years to being one who seeks to serve wherever the need may be, one called to be of service to the people of God.

Lastly, a word of thanks to all I have attempted to serve these many years: the parishioners and college students, the friends and colleagues, and those unfortunate enough to have sat next to me at my local pub for many years. I even tried to evangelize others while having a pint or two, or eight! The church does exist to evangelize wherever we are, and we are called to reach out to others always.

CHAPTER 2

Today's Challenges

In many of the parish settings, I have been asked to fulfill the duties within a written job description, but ministry stretches far beyond mere words within the confines of such a job description. You are engaged in people's lives as they give birth, as they live their lives, and as they prepare to die and everything in between. Ministry is about the womb to the tomb, and that gets messy.

You are with people in times of their great joy and in times of their profound losses and the grief that follows. And that is messy as well. You are there to challenge others personally and professionally to grow in their faith while being challenged as well. That partnership is ministry.

It is never a top-down approach to others. It is a true relational alliance with others that not all can do, let alone even embrace, as an approach to ministry. This has been my approach to ministry and perhaps my approach to all life as well: to see others as coequals along life's journey and to help them seek the God within them, the God beyond them, and the God all around them. That is ministry at its best.

A single negative experience at a young formative age could have ruined every hope I had for my life. Abuse of any kind leaves both a visible and an invisible residue that never goes away completely. These scars can make you cautious in life, in all important relationships, and in every aspect of your being.

Scars can be that constant reminder that someone had done something bad and inappropriate to you. Scars can also remind you that you have survived an ordeal, however brief or long it may have lasted, and that you were made better through your own inventory of resources, your own profound introspection, and your own determination to use the experience as a moment of grace and growth.

Scars, when we are aware of them and their potential for self-understanding, can aide us and guide us through life. You do not recognize this at the time. You survive these moments. You bury them deeply at times. You somehow forget about them for decades or more. Then life unfolds, and you revisit them in light of your new understanding of past events. You have grown and turned a negative experience into an opportunity to contribute something good to an organization and to society as well with the help of God.

My story is not unique. I am certain that others have known sexual abuse within the context of the Catholic Church yet still remain fully engaged in that church to make her a better and safer place for the people of God. I don't know the number of survivors who remain active Catholics, but it's an honorable group who seek reform, change, correction, justice, and reparations—as if!

In these thirty-five-plus years, carrying deeply within me the story and experience of abuse, I arrived at a time and place in my ministerial career when we all watched in horror in the early 2000s the public outing of the clergy-abuse scandal in the Archdiocese of Boston and well beyond Boston too. It was a universal crisis.

I remained engaged in ministry because I knew that not all priests I've known and served with over the years, not all religious brothers and sisters in parishes where I've served alongside them, and not all laypeople I've ministered to and with acted upon the inappropriate attraction toward children and adolescents.

I was serving in a parish on 9/11 when people sought out their local church and all houses of worship for comfort, peace, and solace. I was proud to be a representative of a local parish church at that time when the church was needed most by individuals and families from the parish, other communities, and the nation as a whole. We saw houses of worship for people of every faith coming together in

churches, mosques, and synagogues—faith as the foundational healing element and the church at her very best.

The Boston Marathon bombing was another moment when
people sought the face of God, seeking answers to questions that
simply had no commonsense answers. The church offered a place to
discern those questions of how and why and offer some solace as best
she could. We kept vigil with those who needed the confines of the
church buildings, and the staff and parishioners being together in a
common time of need—that is ministry at its best.

We endured a series of church closings as the church discovered,
finally, that less than 12 percent of Catholics attend services now and
that all the churches we built in the 1950s and 1960s are no longer
needed, especially in the inner cities like Boston and in other large
cities across the country as well.

People migrated to our Boston shores for generations, with
each ethnic group building their own ethnic parishes in and around
Boston proper. As people prospered, they left their inner-city dwell-
ings for the sprawl of the suburbs, and many simply stopped going
to church altogether, as did their children and grandchildren. We
overbuilt!

Church closings in all dioceses is a painful process and an
ordeal for all involved. How it is managed can help ease the pain
of loss to some degree, or it can add fuel to the emotional upheaval
of change. I have witnessed the pain, the hurt, and the anger from
people when a church closes, and I have witnessed individuals who
have been comforted and allowed to express their grief in a healthy
manner. Compassionate leadership is required at these times of loss
and rebuilding.

The COVID-19 pandemic has created havoc, death, and
destruction to all parts of the world. The church world was shut
down completely in ways never known before to her in this country.
Yet the people needed the comfort found in their houses of worship. Yes, we can all be with God in our private spaces or watch the
Mass on television, but that weekly or daily pilgrimage to the local
church, a mosque, a synagogue, etc. offers the people of God the
comfort they seek during cataclysmic times. The communal aspect

of faith is always an essential element of seeking and finding comfort in community.

The church has had to reinvent herself—as she must do often—to be present to the people of God. We've had to find new ways to allow people in churches while being safe. It was, and continues to be, a challenge, but it remains so worth the efforts of many. Slowly our houses of worship are reopening, yet dire predictions tell us 25 to 40 percent of Catholics will not return to church on Sundays. How do we address that spiritual and financial crisis that is upon the horizon?

Working closely with local public health authorities in cities and towns, churches found ways to allow a few people in at a time for private prayer and devotional activity. Closing doors and praying the virus away did not seem like a smart leadership choice. *We needed to be creative then and now!*

Finding a middle road without putting people in harm's way has worked well for many. In time, we have been allowed to celebrate once again Word and sacrament to a limited but now growing number of people. With technology as it is these days, we're also livestreaming church services that are seen by thousands. While TV Mass is nice, the communal dimension of church is missing. Yes, there is spiritual communion. We will see more churches close in days to come. We reinvented the church during the COVID-19 crisis, but will the faithful return, or are they gone forever?

The Black Lives Matter movement(s), along with the protests that followed around the world, has picked at the scab of race issues that has never been fully addressed at all, really. Slavery and what has followed for hundreds of years remains our nations' original sin.

Peaceful protests universally raise awareness for brief moments in time. Riots and looting deflect the focus of the systemic need for change, upheaval, and a replacement of the old ways of doing things. We've made some progress, but where are we really? We've come so far, but so much more needs to be done.

All our faith-based communities of every denomination must be working for change—change that will take generations to see any repair and correction of the sins from our past. Faith communities must be vigilant to include all voices to help lead a society beyond a brief news cycle, beyond a few weeks and months of headlines to fully engage all parts of the system—educational reform, housing reform in inner cities, full and equal employment and voting rights, politics that represent all voices, and so much more—to discern and bring into creation a new way of being a multiracial society where all lives truly matter. It is time to do the hard work required of a civilized nation, assuming we grow our civility.

The 2020 presidential election and what led up to that next-defining moment in history added far more hate to the equation than what peaceful discourse could have provided a nation. A nation simmering over with a fear of the other, a fear of real and imagined threats, and a fear of self-destruction has become the by-product of a nation at war with itself. Healing and reconciliation between political parties, between family members who fight over politics, and between what color of skin to trust, what creed to support, and what news source to follow have made life harder for too many. A nation at its boiling point has more to fear from itself than an attack from a perceived enemy. The enemy is within, and they have arrived.

These are some of the issues facing leaders of organizations today and into the future. Political and religious leaders must muddle through the truth to direct its energies and resources into problem-solving. Burying, obscuring, or dismissing the past only leads to more pain, more chaos, more confusion, more mistrust, and more loss of faith in leaders and the organizations they represent.

This book is merely my viewpoint alone of what happened, what did not happen, what could have happened, and what should be happening going forward. I love my church and will continue to serve her in some lesser role well beyond my retirement from ministry. I firmly believe the Catholic faith is not the only way to know and to serve God but is merely a way that works for me currently.

The challenges of yesteryear, of today, and of tomorrow invite each of us to be reshaped as we attempt to reshape society on a variety of levels. So much reshaping must take place on the political front with race relations and within our faith communities. We must reshape our views of the "other" in our common society. We need not fear the other because of race, gender, nationality, creed, etc.!

I could be a very good practicing Christian, Jew, Muslim, Buddhist, etc. if it were not for the sacraments of the Catholic faith. These ritualistic pathways to the sacred are important to me and for all Catholics and future Catholics, and believe it or not, there are some!

This book does not answer questions; it merely presents experiences of one lay minister who got to live his dream every day serving the people of God in a variety of ways in a variety of cities and towns. I thank all the people at the many parishes where I was fortunate to serve: St. Ann's in Somerville, Massachusetts; Our Lady Comforter of the Afflicted in Waltham, Massachusetts; Saint Boniface in Lunenburg, Massachusetts; Holy Angels in Plaistow, New Hampshire; Corpus Christi—St. Bernard in Newton, Massachusetts; and the Parish of the Transfiguration in Wilmington, Massachusetts.

Also thanks to the many college students I taught at Emmanuel College in Boston, Massachusetts. All of you in each setting taught me a great deal. I hope I helped you in your faith journey as much as you guided me in my journey to date. I was reshaped often with each encounter.

I have to thank a religious sister and former principal, Sr. Kathy Carr, CSJ, who once invited me into her office to assist with a school project. A simple invitation was, for me, an evangelizing moment that led to a vocation in the Catholic Church all these many years. The best way to evangelize, to come and see, is what is needed these days. Come and see, be open to being reshaped!

CHAPTER 3

No Father Figure

My father died at the age of forty-eight years old. He was a smoker, and according to family lore, he had a series of heart attacks over a five-year period that took its toll on him ultimately. Had he lived in more current times, there probably would have been a treatment and/or a cure for his heart ailments.

Not having a dad seemed the norm for me. I was two years old when he died. My sisters were six and nine. My mother was a widow at the age of thirty. Difficult times forced her to play the dual roles of mother and father. Certainly an unfair load to carry at her young age.

Growing up in a tight-knit neighborhood allowed me the opportunity to see other family models and dynamics. Most had the mother-father model, some had divorced moms raising kids, and there were some never-married parents and single individuals.

My extended family on the maternal side offered me a variety of uncles, male cousins, and other male figures whom I might have been able to turn to for a type of male influence in my life, but all these men had others who looked to them for guidance and support. At some point, I had the attitude that I will simply figure things out on my own someday, and I continue to do so today.

The paternal side of the family was an unknown gift to me until I was a middle-aged adult for reasons still unclear to me. When my father died, so did the connections to his family. What the reasons were remain a mystery and unknown to me. Why my mother didn't speak of them or why they didn't stay in touch are questions that don't require answers. I'm delighted to have them in my life today at long last.

My childhood home, while somber most of the time, was a home that provided food, shelter, and the necessities of daily life for three young children. While we were never lavished with gifts at birthdays or Christmas, we got just what we needed. The Christmas tree for many years was a subdued and grim reminder of loss and grief with a limited number of sparkling lights rather than a presentation of a festive time. We did not want to appear too happy, I guess, to Santa.

Forced to work two jobs at times, my mother leaned on my older sisters to manage the household at their young and tender ages of six and nine. We all had tasks and chores each day, typical of the times. My sisters cooked and cleaned. I eventually had garbage duties with the task of taking out and taking in the trash barrels each week. I guess trash was the manly task of the day.

As I got older, I would have loved the opportunity to have a dad or a dad figure to lean on, to ask questions, to look up to in admiration, and to just hang with. My childhood home was directly across the street from the neighborhood park, and I loved and played sports daily. It was easy to roll out of bed, throw on some clothes, grab a bat and glove, and find a group of friends to play with. We had basketball courts and baseball fields—more like dirt, rocks, and broken glass than a plush green grass field to play on.

Among those individuals I admired then were the Little League coaches, the older kids who invited me to play ball with them, and in the summer months, I admired the recreation leaders who gathered kids every day from 9:00 a.m. to 3:00 p.m., engaging us in a variety of sports and other activities.

By the time I reached the teen years, my interest in sports was waning just enough to allow thoughts of the opposite sex to enter my teen brain. I had questions about females that I would never bring home to my sisters. It did not seem appropriate at the time, nor did I trust my feelings and emotions to another. My circle of male friends was the epicenter for all knowledge about the opposite sex. It was the best I could do at that time.

My mother, at some point, decided that I needed to talk with someone about such matters. Perhaps it is a maternal thing that single moms raising sons are forced to seek out the best resources available to her to assist with child-rearing and the more sensitive matters far too delicate for the mother-son relationship to discuss.

At about fourteen years old, I was brought to the family doctor. I wasn't sick. I had no fever, no runny nose, no mumps, no chicken pox, no rubella, or anything else that might have required a doctor visit. We didn't do yearly physicals back then; you saw the doctor only when you were ill. I wasn't ill!

I was called from the waiting room to go into the doctor's office. He asked me if I had any questions or if anything was bothering me. He kept probing me to open up—about what, I had no clue. Finally, he asked me if I had any questions about sex. Then it hit me: I was having the sex talk with the family doctor!

I could feel the embarrassment and rage moving up from within. Within seconds, I politely told the doctor I was fine and abruptly left the office to walk home—eventually hours later.

In retrospect, it was a harmless moment where a mother didn't know how to talk to a son about such a sensitive topic. It would have made her uncomfortable, and perhaps she knew it would have made me feel uneasy as well. But there is more to this aspect of the relationship that I will share in the next chapters.

I knew almost nothing of my dad's history, his family, Irish heritage, etc. Who was this man I was named after? I did not know much about him until much later in life, when I learned that he grew up in South Boston, Massachusetts, in a staunchly Irish Catholic neighborhood. I discovered too that he dropped out of school at sixteen years old to go to work to help in the support of his ten siblings.

I found out he was considered "old" when he enlisted in the army at the age of thirty-two, served in WWII, was later injured back on US soil, and spent time at Walter Reed General Hospital in Washington, DC, where a pin was placed on his knee. He was honorably discharged from the army in 1944. That was a man who had leadership skills to serve his family in need and a nation at war.

An image was being created in my mind of the man I could never call out to as "dad." In my thirties, having gained more knowledge of my father's genealogy and my own, I discovered the names of his siblings (my aunts and uncles and their children). I learned the names of his parents (my grandparents). His father came from Lettermore in County Galway—a place I would eventually visit for purely sentimental reasons.

I was able to go back even deeper into the Griffin roots in Ireland, finding a fifth great-grandfather in the county of Galway in 1798. These genealogical discoveries were quite enriching and emotional as well. I now had a sense of where the Irish roots began and where I came from as well.

My mother's roots were 100 percent Italian, and as children, we had a connection to that heritage through the meals, breads, pastries, music, wine, family gatherings, etc. Our Italian grandparents lived with us for a brief time prior to their deaths, although I was too young to recall them. The Italian language was used often in the house when my mother did not want us to know what was going on in a conversation.

The parish church was a "national" parish where a few generations of Italians built their tiny yet magnificent house of worship. My next-door neighbors were Italian as well. The smells, language, food, etc. made me feel Italian. From my youthful understanding and naïveté of my background, I assumed I was 100 percent Italian—until I discovered I was much more!

With the knowledge of my father's siblings' names, I wanted to reach out to them somehow. I did not know how many were still alive, who died, where they lived, or if they even knew I existed. I wanted to pick up the telephone and introduce myself to the family. It was not until I saw the death notice of my father's last surviving sister, Mary (Griffin) Amirault, in a Boston newspaper on a Sunday morning when I decided that I needed to reach out to introduce myself.

I waited a few weeks to pass after her death to begin this quest to meet and know my dad's family. My first thought was *Who wants to hear from me in the throes of loss, grief, a wake, and funeral?* We still had telephone books in the 1980s, so looking up names and phone numbers was a simple task. I came upon the names of cousins still living in South Boston. Some had migrated to the South Shore of Massachusetts, also known as the Irish Riviera.

Three cousins in particular were the most welcoming individuals I've come across in my lifetime. My dad's nieces were thrilled to hear from me. They knew I existed but hadn't a clue where I lived or what had become of me. We talked for hours and eventually agreed to a get-together, which led to a few large family reunions. The meeting of my dad's nieces, cousins, and extended family gave me a better sense of him, of where he came from, and where I came from as well. It's been a very satisfying and ongoing relationship that continues today with calls and letters and occasional visits.

Finding my roots metaphorically gave me a sense of my Irish roots—they were quite common to the Italian heritage! Both sets of grandparents were looking for opportunity in a new land. Some fled oppression, violence, fascism, and their own unique versions of discrimination.

Discovering one's roots humbles oneself. These individuals took leaps of faith that remain common with new people arriving today in this country. All are seeking a better way of life—a chance to be reshaped by the opportunities that do not exist elsewhere.

CHAPTER 4

The Abusive Encounter

The year 1967 was supposed to be a magical year for me as a Boston sports fan. That summer, I wore my Carl Yastrzemski T-shirt nearly every day on the ball field across the street from my childhood home.

The Boston Red Sox finally made it to the World Series that year and faced the formidable St. Louis Cardinals; Jim Lonborg versus Bob Gibson; Yaz versus Orlando Cepeda; even the managerial matchup was Hall of Fame—like, Red Schoendienst versus Dick Williams.

The Celtics nearly won another NBA championship that year. The Patriots won just three games, but that was considered a good season back in the day. The Bruins were good but not good enough and were eliminated in the playoffs once again by the dreaded Montreal Canadiens.

Bobby Orr was just a kid himself in 1967, but his influence on the sport would soon follow as we witnessed hockey rinks being built in numerous cities throughout the metro Boston area. Street hockey quickly became a sport played year-round in the neighborhoods upon Orr's arrival on the scene.

The year 1967 was also the approximate time when I began to be intrigued by a church vocation: God calling me somewhere to serve the church. I did not really know the word *vocation* as an eleven-year-old, but I knew there was a certain mystique about a life in which I felt uniquely at home in my parish church.

The "smells and bells" of that tiny church only added to the mystique. Church was the place where I wanted to live out my baptismal vocation in the world as I reflect back upon those days. Had things gone in another direction, I might have been a priest today!

I was fortunate enough to live in an area of town where I could attend a small ethnic parish just two blocks from my home. It is where I was baptized and celebrated the other sacraments of initiation.

I also had the option of attending a much-larger territorial parish just up the hill from the six-family dwelling where I grew up. The larger of the two parishes is where I played CYO basketball. While I attended the local public elementary school with many of my neighborhood friends, I had other friends who attended the parochial schools in the neighborhood.

Summers were that special time of the year to reconnect with all these individuals to play a pickup game of the seasonal sports at the local park. Summer was baseball season played on one of the grassless and dusty fields across the street from my house. Fall was the time for street football or basketball played at the park or in one of the schoolyards.

By the time I turned sixteen, a skating rink was built across the street from my house. I quickly learned how to ice-skate and had my first paying job at that same rink as a skate guard yelling at my peers to keep skating rather than just hanging out in a corner of the rink. Being a young boy at that time was mostly a great experience, and when I look back on those days of having no responsibilities—it was magical!

The mystique of my "home" church was multifaceted for me. It began with the building. It was a weekly pilgrimage even though it was just two blocks to the red brick church. A climb up the stairs that seemed like four hundred steps to a child, when in reality it was probably just twenty steps at best.

Entering this sacred space, one would immediately encounter the smell of real candles, the dark wooden pews, a sanctuary area that was segregated by an altar rail with a mosaiclike crucifix looking out over the pews, and the *assembly*—another word that I didn't really know or understand at that time.

There were always six to eight nuns—the good Sisters of Notre Dame—at every Mass on the weekends, typically in the front pews in the full habit of that bygone era. The mystique of that church also included the kneeling widows dressed in black from head to toe praying the rosary faithfully every Sunday before Mass had started, during the Mass, and long after the Mass had ended—and always in Italian.

The mystique included the organ prelude music before mass, the entrance procession, the celebration of the Word and sacrament in a foreign language (I could never differentiate between the Latin or the Italian), the orderly procession to the Eucharist, and the lining up on our knees at the altar rail to receive Corpus Christi, the body of Christ.

The mystique did not end there. There was a lower church that was always dark with a low ceiling, stone walls, and confessionals adorned with those dark-red velvetlike curtains. Real votive candles, not like today's battery-operated ones, were always burning at both sides of the sanctuary just behind the altar rail. A gate allowed for safe passage to these candles.

My home parish, like others then, had standing room—only masses. There were plenty of priests to celebrate the Mass and administer the sacraments. There were plenty of nuns to educate the local youth and help maintain a healthy parish life. The Catholic Church was vibrant in 1967.

The parish parochial school was the primary recruitment center for future altar servers, and on occasion, we public school boys would be considered as well for training to serve at Masses. I was one of those neighborhood boys invited to be trained to serve. As my memory recalls, it was the first of two consecutive Saturday mornings in mid- to late September when I arrived at the church for training.

The air of mystique I felt about the church was somehow inching me closer to sorting out whatever "ministerial calling" I was feeling to be more engaged with the church. Something was nudging me toward church—an inner and an outer force, or a voice, whispering me forward.

Did I really have a vocation at eleven years old? I thought I might have had one, but I lacked the ability to verbalize or discern or even discuss with anyone what I was thinking or feeling at that time.

Rather than going into the church for altar-server training upon my arrival, I was greeted and encouraged by a senior altar server to come to the rectory for a meeting with the parish priests. Maybe it was an initial meeting for the priests to get to know me better as I was a public school student. Or perhaps something else was going on in the church at the time. A funeral? A wedding? I really did not know. I just went along, being eleven years old.

I was invited to the second floor of the residence. I was directed to the pastor's bedroom next. He was a much-beloved figure in the parish. Originally from Italy and called to serve a parish made up of mostly families of Italian heritage, with some Irish thrown into the mix as well. Was I simply and innocently getting a tour of the rectory? Not really!

I was told to sit on the bed. I was then directed to pull down my pants. Before I complied, something inside me said, "Get out of here."

Nothing else happened that morning. I left quickly running down the stairs toward the front door of the rectory and out to the sidewalk. Within just a few seconds fled another boy from the neighborhood. The same look of confusion, a little bit of fear, and the same dose of shame that I was feeling appeared on his face as well. We never talked, then or ever, about what happened to us that morning. He died several years ago.

The mystique, however, did not fade away for me that Saturday morning. Perhaps it should have ended whatever *calling* or *vocation* I was considering at that time. I really wanted to be an altar server. There was a rapport between the neighborhood youth and the priests and nuns of the parish that I had admired, and maybe even longed for.

My father died when I was just two years old, and I had no male role model or influence in my life outside of two uncles, a few male cousins, and some friends' dads from the neighborhood. The parish priests were the only real male figures in my life who I saw often during the week—in the park and schoolyards, at church, at CCD, and even in the homes of a few neighbors for Sunday dinners.

Often, the priests could be seen shooting hoops at the local basketball court. The nuns could be found skipping rope with the girls of the neighborhood. There was even a very youngish Notre Dame nun who could shoot a basketball better than most of the boys. She may have been my first crush!

The very next Saturday, I arrived at the rectory again, seeking to be trained as an altar server. What was I thinking? The invite upstairs took place once again. I followed behind the beloved pastor. I entered his bedroom. I was directed to remove my pants and underwear, and I obeyed.

Another priest entered the room with a camera—the old-fashioned type of camera with the flashbulb at the top. While one priest stroked and fondled me and orally manipulated me, the other was taking photos.

I do not recall how long this attack lasted, probably just a few minutes at best, but at some point, I knew this was not an appropriate behavior. I felt horrible about myself immediately. I never ejaculated—at eleven years old, I did not really have a clue what that was. I was never penetrated. I never had to perform a sexual act on either of those two clerics. I am extremely fortunate compared to the brutality experienced by many others locally and across our church world today. It truly was deviant and criminal behavior.

Running from that rectory (again) and out onto the sidewalk (again), I never looked back as I did the previous Saturday. I did not wait this time to see if anyone else would be running behind me in shame and confusion, feeling guilty or filled with fear.

I recall hearing some noises as I passed another room with closed doors on the second floor of the rectory—moans and groans perhaps. Were there other victims? I had no proof, and I did not want to wait around for any proof. It was time to run home to safety—or so I thought.

I ran home to share this experience with an expectation that my mother would be a source of comfort. I honestly cannot recall if I shared it immediately, within minutes or hours or even within a few days. It was fifty-plus years ago. That part of the story remains a little fuzzy to me. I do know that it was indeed shared, and her reaction was not what I had desired, needed, nor what I had expected, and her reaction impacted the mother-son relationship for the next fifty years. She died in 2018.

Sharing the story with her felt strange and so very uncomfortable. How does an eleven-year-old boy share such a story with his mother? I felt some level of relief as the words were flowing from my mouth, but that relief quickly turned to shame, to confusion, and eventually to anger as my mother did not believe, would not believe, or could not believe what I was saying to her.

Before I could finish the details of what had happened to me, I was silenced. I was told to "shut up." I was told two contradictory statements as well—first, it never happened, and second, if it did, I misunderstood what had happened. That never made any sense to me. How do you misunderstand the actions of those two priests?

My mother reinforced again and again in that brief encounter that I would never say a bad word about these two priests to anyone at any time. That was the beginning of the end of my relationship with her. It was always a fractured relationship that spilled onto my relationship with my sisters and other family members as well throughout my life.

My mother lost her husband, my father, to heart disease after just twelve years of marriage. She had three young children to raise alone after his death, with me being the youngest. I am certain her hands were full, and she was indeed overwhelmed by the prospects of life without her partner. She worked two jobs at times just to pay the rent, to buy food, to pay the bills—all the things a parent must do.

She was angry at God as she saw God being the responsible one for my father's death. My father had heart disease. She must have expected God to intervene and offer a cure. God did not intervene. She got mad at God. God was an easy target of her pain and suffering, I get that!

Being mad at God, I imagine, led to her decision to part ways with the church, yet her children would need to attend Mass each week, go to Sunday school, and receive their sacraments. I am glad she did that for me. Today, I remain the only one of the three children who attends Mass faithfully. She would occasionally attend the Sunday "priest dinners" in the neighborhood, however.

As I reflect upon that now, I see that was her only way of maintaining some connection to the Holy Mother Church and to God. As someone who has served in ministry now for more than three decades, I have witnessed how very common this reaction is with people who lose loved ones: we blame God, and we no longer practice our faith.

The mystique of the church continued to remain within me. I never wanted to be an altar boy again. That call ended abruptly. If being an altar server would have been the pathway to the priesthood for me someday, that road to the seminary and eventual ordination and a lifelong commitment to that vocation was also now at a dead end.

After the abuse, I would continue to go to Mass each week at my home parish, but I would sit in the very last pew or stand in the back with the ushers. Upon receiving Communion, I would flee the building. Today, when I see people do that, I am always troubled when they leave before the Mass has even ended. They have their reasons for leaving, I am quite certain. But leaving Mass before it concludes with the great commissioning, sent into the world to be disciples for others? I try each day to embrace those words!

Once the sacrament of confirmation was celebrated, I did take a brief hiatus from attending Mass for about eight years, from the ages of fourteen to twenty-two. The rule of the house was, as it is sadly today with many families, get confirmed and then you can decide to stop going to church. It is a graduation mentality: you have now completed your studies, and you can decide what you want to believe and how you will practice those beliefs. This is a deeply flawed understanding and theology of the sacrament that continues today, sadly, in many parish programs. It's about initiation and not about graduation!

The bad experience of what was supposed to be altar-server training did not taint my view of the church nor my view of God.

Those two priests—among the many, as we now know—should have been held accountable for their criminal actions at that time.

I failed to go forward immediately after these two events out of fear, perhaps: fear of not being believed again, fear of being ridiculed by others, or perhaps just fear of something else I can't really fully understand.

I know I was not the only victim from that parish. A website naming the parish and naming the religious-order priests that staffed the parish has been detailing the many accounts of abuse both locally and nationally.

I've been following that website for many years now, and that has given me the affirmation knowing I was not alone, knowing others filed abuse claims, knowing that others held them accountable even though I couldn't come forward with a complaint.

I was not the only victim in the Boston archdiocese or the universal church in the world. These two extremely flawed clerics—among the many, both criminals—never deprived me of the passion for the church's mission in our society and in the world, nor did they prevent me from playing a small part in that mission that is rooted in our common baptism.

The victims of clergy sexual abuse—more accurately the church's abuse scandal, for it was not just priests—reshaped countless people into being suicide statistics, alcohol-and-drug statistics, and abusers-themselves statistics. What were their young dreams before their assaults? What did they want to be when they grew up?

Many never got to grow up. Many never recovered. Many barely get by spiritually, emotionally, etc. Many remain broken.

CHAPTER 5

Transformation of Self

Fat Tom was a hideous yet accurate nickname I assigned to myself to offer some self-deprecating humor about my girth. My weight never bothered me entirely, but it probably formed ideas about me in the minds of others: Could he do the work with all the excess weight? Is he an appealing leader while being a sweaty pile of goo? Do fat people have any real value to an organization? Is he always thinking about pizza, éclairs, cake, bagels, pretzels, pies?

Nobody ever posed these questions out loud in my company, but we know first impressions matter in life. Fat Tom may know his stuff, but look at him! He's always a sweaty man! We can't help forming these first impressions of others when we meet them—fat people, tall people, short people, black people, brown people, old people, young people, and all those other people we encounter daily in life. We form opinions of the other, and it remains embedded in our psyches.

Food was my preference to numb myself. Food would momentarily give me that high to briefly enjoy life and bury whatever the pain of the past may have been. Moments after a pizza was consumed, moments after the Chinese food containers were emptied, those buried feelings would resurface. No amount of food can erase the hurts of the past—but I tried with food.

In 2011, I decided Fat Tom needed to go away, vanish from society, so I entered a weight-loss program that would teach me proper nutrition, diet, exercise, etc., all with the end goal of gastric bypass surgery. I was required to show initiative to change my life for the better by dropping a small percentage of weight within a three-month period. I met the program goal, and surgery would be scheduled.

Fat Tom was prediabetic and had high blood pressure and sleep apnea, and God knows what other time bombs were ticking away within my fatness—not an attractive future for a man in his early fifties.

The surgery took place on Valentine's Day, and it was the first time I got myself a gift for such a holiday: an opportunity to live a long, happy, and healthy life.

The first day postsurgery was brutal. The surgical gas hadn't escaped the body completely, so there was intense upper-body pain from the residual surgical gas. I was able to walk and move about almost immediately after the surgery.

A limited diet for the first weeks of Jell-O, water, sugar-free popsicles, and plain yogurt was a great start to the initial weight loss. I no longer craved food, no longer wanted to look at food, and to this day, looking at an Easter or Thanksgiving banquet, or any other celebration featuring an enormous banquet of food, leaves me feeling quite nauseous.

So the first year or so, you drop a crazy amount of poundage, provided you remain rigid to portion control, eating proper foods, and exercise. I found walking and biking to be the easiest, the most enjoyable, and worked for me. Everyone is different, but adhering to the weight-loss plan post-gastric bypass surgery is a must.

As the pounds melt away, you begin to feel a sense of newfound energy, and for someone who always had a large ego, you begin to see yourself in a different light—and others do too, I'm certain. Always bordering on cocky and arrogant, my self-esteem skyrocketed. A "now-thinner Tom" was a force to be reckoned with in ministry.

As I entered ministerial life in the mid-1980s, first as a catechist and later as a director of some very large faith formation programs, I lacked the educational background and degree, the formation of self, the needed credentials, the knowledge, and any real experience whatsoever to really be doing what I was doing. My peers were certified in one field of ministry or another, and I was out of my league those first few years.

It was time to determine if this was going to be my chosen career, my ministerial future: to be a certified and credentialed lay ecclesial minister in the Catholic Church. I discerned my next steps, and it led me to Emmanuel College in Boston, Massachusetts.

The college had an adult-learner program that took into consideration past work and life experiences that could be considered creditworthy. I was able to get a jump-start in my pursuit of a BA that really excited me and challenged me simultaneously. From the days of being the class clown throughout middle school and high school, I suddenly became a sponge for knowledge in religious studies, psychology, political science, and philosophy. I was excited to learn for the first time in my life.

It took nearly three years to complete my BA in religious studies and psychology. I went to classes early in the morning and after work, and took weekend and summer classes and whatever else was presented to me to hasten receiving the degree. I thought once I received the BA I'd be content and ready to be credentialed to do what I was doing in ministry. Emmanuel College lit a fire within me that led me to enroll at the Weston Jesuit School of Theology in Harvard Square, Cambridge, Massachusetts. What was I thinking?

Weston not only had the theological and biblical heavyweights teaching classes but also had people from around the world in leadership positions and who happened to be on sabbatical in the area and would audit classes. I was out of my league, I thought, in these classes, but I held on to a newfound dream to pursue a theological degree—what I would do with that, I hadn't a clue!

The Weston experience was quite profound studying with the global church community. It opened my eyes to issues of people around the world. It grounded me in liturgical studies and pastoral presence. I furthered my biblical understanding of OT and NT studies. It shaped my own spiritual personhood as I met with a spiritual director often during my time there. The community liturgies were some of the most profound experiences of worship I've ever attended. I was reshaped by these two places: Emmanuel and Weston.

Being "reshaped" physically and spiritually gave me opportunities to now be more fully engaged in ministry, with a sense of being respected for academic accomplishments and paying attention to my health for the first time. Doors that I perceived as closing now felt as if they were flung open to me, giving me more visibility in the parishes I served, in a college setting, at the diocesan level, and beyond as well.

I was invited to return to Emmanuel College to become an adjunct faculty member in their Religious Studies department. Teaching side by side with former professors was inspiring, to say the least. Teaching college freshmen and sophomores was inspiring as well. They challenged belief systems and challenged my beliefs as I attempted to make them go deeper into their faith development. At the end of the semesters, professors are typically assessed by the students. Half thought I was too pro-Catholic while the other half thought I was too anti-Catholic. I think I did my job.

Being "reshaped" in a variety of ways added to my already large understanding of self and my self-confidence. I never thought I was less than; rather, I knew I needed more self-development to excel in my chosen path. I went on to lead large faith formation programs in a variety of parish settings, led retreats, formed parishes in their planning for years and decades to come, assisted with the canonical merger of parishes, and have pretty much done everything there is to do in parish life outside of sacramental celebrations—I know my limitations!

Transformation of self is an essential component of leadership regardless of the job, profession, calling, etc. One must recognize early what is needed from oneself to enter a field, excel in that field, and continue to examine one's ongoing needs to remain in that field.

I was a truck driver at one time who felt a calling to serve God and others. Had I not listened to that calling, that inner whisper, I'd still be driving a truck and being the best driver that I could be delivering products for companies. My transformation introduced me to something I once dreamed of but never thought I was worthy to serve. Yes, I still question my worthiness!

Chapter 6

My Son's Death

December 10, 2018, was the darkest of emotional days I had ever experienced in my life. I received a midafternoon phone call from my daughter's husband asking me to rush to the hospital because my son suffered a heart attack. What? Who? When? How?

Within just a few minutes was a second call saying it was too late. My son was dead, and all I could do was scream without a sound coming from me in my empty house. Tom Junior was dead at thirty-nine years old!

As a teen, I had always wanted a son—in many ways for selfish reasons—to have that father-son relationship that I never experienced. If I couldn't have a dad growing up, I could become a dad later in life. Seemed logical at that time.

I had it all planned out in my head to have a son someday without even knowing who would be his mother. There was no thought of a daughter yet because I needed a son; more accurately, I needed the father-son relationship.

With me eventually getting married at twenty-two, my first wife and I proceeded to have our first child within ten months of the wedding, and she knew well in advance that she would produce a male child and he'd be named after me and my father. Luckily, her father and brother shared my first and middle names, so everyone was happy with the name Thomas Joseph for my son.

The nine months of anticipation for this son to come into the world, the notion of being a father with a son, and all the restoration of the past with those feelings of emptiness would be eradicated in that sacred moment of birth, I imagined. That very moment watching a child gush and spill into the world is a memory that has stayed with me forever. Holding my son for the first time, I felt something that I'd never experienced before: pure ecstasy.

There could be no better feeling of having a son come into the world that you had envisioned since being a teenager, until an amazing daughter is born fifty weeks later—Irish twins!

And so I was a dad to Tom Junior. Somehow, missing out on the father-son relationship was now reversed and fixed. Whatever I missed out on was now going to be played out with my son. I imagined we would bond through playing baseball, fishing, watching sports together, just hanging out, and talking about everything imaginable. And we did for many years.

When his mother and I divorced years later, the father-son relationship was reshaped dramatically as his mother remarried, and now a stepfather was in the picture doing all the things with my son that I had always envisioned. As my son and his mother moved farther and farther away geographically, I could feel him emotionally slipping away as well, as that bond we once had was slowly and steadily eroding.

I recognized that he was growing into a young man who eventually would be creating a family of his own someday. He would have the same dreams I once had about being a dad to a son—but that dream was cut short by his sudden death.

He eventually did meet the love of his life, Nicole, who wowed him enough at first sight that he knew he would marry her someday. When you see your future, grab hold of her!

We had our challenges as father and son, our joys and sorrows together and apart, but at least for some all-too-brief time, I had that father-son relationship in my life that I had craved and that remains today even in his death. I remember the conversations we used to have throughout his life, the good and the bad ones, and all the in-between ones.

We argued a lot, especially near the end of his life. I never lived up to his expectations whatever they were. I'm still not sure what I could have done different for him. I've read of the challenges within the father-son relationship, but having no father at a young age, I never felt as if I lived in my father's shadow or that I disappointed him in any way—there was no him to disappoint.

Being a father for the first time allowed me the opportunity to have that unconditional love that you read about, that you dream about, and that you desire from all good relationships. When the call came that my son had died, I was devastated on many levels. The noiseless scream that seemed to go on and on and on for hours eventually subsided—reconciliation was never going to occur for us.

His death reminded me again of my own childhood feelings of loss, emptiness, and loneliness associated with any type of loss. The passing of time has only reinforced the void that has always been there no matter how I try to mask that brutal pain. Years now after his death I continue to get quite sad whenever I think about him. Father's Day, his birthday, watching *The Sopranos* or the Boston Bruins, certain songs by Sinatra—all are reminders of my son.

I seek isolation rather than the company of others when the sadness arrives. Why burden people with my pain? Everyone has enough of their own pain already. My daughter, his widow, his nieces and nephews, his friends all have pain, but a parent's pain is uniquely different—not deeper or worse, just different. You just want to keep yelling in your empty house.

Two important deaths sixty years apart reshaped my world in incredible ways. The loss of a father at such a young age never afforded me a concept of what masculinity might look like. I had uncles in the family, obviously, but whom that I could lean on for direction, questions, etc. I never saw a husband-wife relationship play out at home.

I had distorted views of what fatherhood and married life looked like as it was played out on television in the sixties. *Leave It to Beaver* was idyllic, yet it was a traditional home with two parents. *The Honeymooners* was a crass portrayal of a scheming husband who also happened to be verbally abusive and always threatened physical violence in each episode—to the moon, Alice!

There were very few, if any, television portrayals of a fatherless home featuring a young son being raised by a working mother and two older sisters. I need to figure this out on my own, and I continue in this journey.

My son's death still haunts me daily in extremely raw ways. My dad's death haunts me in a longing way that has become more melancholic than haunting. Two deaths sixty years apart forced me to reshape every aspect of my life, in particular my coping skills related to loss, death, grief, etc.

CHAPTER 7

The Abuse Comes to Light

When the accounts of the far-too-many clergy-abuse cases surfaced locally, nationally, and internationally in the early 2000s, I thought for a very brief moment of adding my name to the long and growing list of victims who were seeking some level of financial compensation and emotional or spiritual support from the Boston archdiocese.

I was working in a parish in another local diocese at that time, and I can still recall the anger, the confusion, and the rage that I was feeling. I read every article published about the victims and the accused priests, and I grew angrier with each story. I chose to stay informed, which just reminded me of the previous assaults on me.

It was beyond my comprehension how my church—*our* church—could allow for the abuse to continue for countless decades and be so complicit in these heinous and criminal acts. Why did I remain not only as a practicing Catholic but also as a lay minister?

It was, and remains still at times, confusing to serve in an organization that hid her secrets so well for such a long time. Was I, am I still being complicit to remain?

For a moment, I thought of contacting that high-profile attorney who seemed to be the voice and the face of the victims and the survivors. I thought adding my name to the growing list of victims would lend some level of support to those who were harmed physically, emotionally, and spiritually.

I reconsidered that stance quickly as I didn't want to be identified as another victim or survivor. I also didn't want to be paraded in front of cameras nor answer any hard questions from reporters. I didn't feel that I needed to do that. I don't feel I need that today either! Other victims could frown upon my lack of action or chastise me for being indifferent to their plight, but I did what I had to do in order to move forward with my life.

I never sought any therapy or counseling earlier in life as I felt I was doing more than "okay" outside of the occasional anger that surfaced when those accounts of abuse were finally made public. I didn't need, nor did I want, any notoriety associated with the ongoing clergy abuse scandal. I wasn't looking for a financial settlement of any kind.

Perhaps my rationale or justification has always been focused on the level of the abuse. I wasn't raped, nor was I asked to perform any sexual acts on a priest. Others needed to be compensated and needed short-term and/or long-term therapy for what happened to them. I simply wanted to move forward, and I continue to move forward.

The experience of attempting to tell this story to my mother taught me a very distorted message about relationships early in my life: to keep my experiences, my feelings, my thoughts, and my emotions private. Never communicate openly or honestly in important relationships. Hide your feelings and emotions—not a good formula or foundation for any important and lasting relationship.

I took that very approach into every early relationship I had with members of the opposite sex. I never allowed any female to get too close to me where I might become vulnerable, open, or willing to share my feelings. Nobody was going to get inside my head or my heart. That approach led to several early dysfunctional relationships as a teenager and young adult, and I take full responsibility for all that.

Obviously, the relationship with my mother was never the same. She never got to know me beyond that eleven-year-old boy with a story of abuse to tell. I always felt like a misfit in my home. I could feel the contempt and disdain—real or imagined—in her looks, the stares, the odd glances my way. Without any proof, I believe at some point in my young life my mother shared this story with my two older sisters and other relatives as well. I've never asked them, to this very day, if they knew of my abuse claim. It no longer seems relevant.

I've never really had a close-enough relationship with either of them to ask if they had heard about what happened to me at eleven years old. I have tried on numerous occasions throughout these many years to have a relationship with each of them, but something always forces a breakdown in the sibling relationship. Our common past has never been addressed!

We never really shared much growing up in the same house, and we don't really know each other as adults today. We never communicated well as a family unit, we mistrusted each other, and we had no bond as siblings. The future could always change the dynamics, but time is running out.

I recall playing CYO basketball on Saturday mornings and Little League baseball games at night in the park directly across the street from my home, yet no family members were ever in attendance. That should have clued me into the sad reality of a dysfunctional homelife.

The female relationships I had as a teenager weren't long-lasting, as each female, I later learned, was warned by my mother, "Move on, he'll never amount to anything." It became an all-too-commonly heard phrase. Perhaps she was merely tipping them off that I might be damaged goods? In spite of those words ringing in my head on occasion, today I consider myself to be successful in many areas of my personal and ministerial life. Still a flawed human being but always being reshaped in new ways.

Chapter 8

Experiences

Fast-forward to today. I've been engaged in lay ecclesial ministry for thirty-five-plus years. I have a BA in religious studies and psychology from Emmanuel College in Boston. I have an MA in theological studies from the former Weston Jesuit School of Theology (now reunited with Boston College School of Theology and Ministry).

I also have postgraduate certificates in spiritual direction and pastoral leadership. I have made a genuine effort to be an effective pastoral leader and minister to and for the people of God through ongoing formation.

I have been an innovative religious education director in three New England dioceses: Boston, Manchester, and Worcester. I was an adjunct professor at Emmanuel College for several years, teaching in their Religious Studies department.

That college teaching experience energized me and gave me a greater awareness of how young people view religion and spirituality today. They don't all fit into the "Religion is very hypocritical" category. Some have such zeal to grow in their faith through a variety of spiritual encounters. While many of us simply memorized facts and dates, young people want to know the whys of religion: "Why do we do certain things in certain ways?"

I have served large-city parishes and small-country parishes. I've worked in single parishes, clustered parishes, reconfigured parishes, and now in multi-parish and stand-alone collaboratives.

I've enjoyed working with children, youth and families, couples preparing for marriage, and individuals who are seeking a declaration of nullity; training liturgical ministers; leading retreats and days of reflection; presiding at wakes and committals; and much more. Outside of celebrating the Mass and administering the sacraments, there isn't much I have not done ministerially in the church. That will continue as long as the passion remains, but fatigue is settling in.

I have remained fully engaged in the leadership of the church at both the parish and archdiocesan levels. My professional development and educational and formational pursuits continue to allow me to be prepared to serve the church and her people into the future, however long that may be.

During the COVID-19 pandemic, I was the point person at the parish handling safety protocols for the safe return of people in our churches and other buildings. The role was nothing that I was trained to "do" or "be," but you treat what is in front of you at that moment, making certain people were safe.

Of late, I have had this feeling of "burnout" as I think about the past year in the world. COVID-19 has caused loss of life, serious illness, lifelong health concerns, etc. It's made some scared to leave home, to shop, to worship, to meet with family and friends. COVID has reshaped our common world.

The emotional toll it has taken on everyone, me included, is to be examined for years to come. How our children have been educated through computer screens will have long-lasting concerns. The frustrations of parents trying to be teachers too has created disharmony in homes.

For me, either because of my long career of thirty-five-plus years, my arrival at age sixty-five, or just a level of frustration with church infrastructure at times has brought me to the burnout question: Am I burned-out? Can I remain an effective leader? Has the time arrived to leave parish ministry?

To be determined!

Chapter 9

Out of the Chaos

Newton, Massachusetts, was a very complex ministerial challenge yet not a unique situation in the early 2000s for a variety of reasons, as many in the Archdiocese of Boston might recall. A parish was to be suppressed, a church sit-in and protest commenced, and letters were written to the cardinal, to Rome, to anyone who would listen to the pleas of the people whose church was closing. TV crews interviewed parishioners picketing in front of the church, something that became commonplace locally and nationally.

Then a reversal of that decision to close the church accompanied the announcement to merge the reopened church with another local parish. It was chaos created at the top but repaired by wise guidance and grassroots efforts by the foot soldiers in parish life: the people and the staff.

The pastoral staff needed to listen and to excel at bringing two different parishes together in worship, in purpose, and in mission. Yes, they were both Catholic parishes, but they had a different socio-economic makeup and different ways of being a church. They had their own unique approaches, styles of worship, cultures, and traditions of living out the mission of the church.

It was very reminiscent of trying to blend two families into a new marriage, with stepchildren and former spouses and former in-laws, each with their own separate identities and each with their own ways of being. That takes time, patience, and lots of work! And it doesn't always mesh.

Different traditions needed to be honored, respected, and celebrated. There were numerous challenges along the way, and they were met patiently over the years, and today, they are a vibrant parish.

One such challenge was a willingness to trust the newly assigned pastor and the staff who were hired. We were seen initially as mere mouthpieces for the archdiocese, but over the course of many months and years, we were eventually embraced, respected, and trusted, and even loved eventually—probably after we left!

We had to allow for the parishioners to grieve what was, to grieve a loss, to honor the memories, to respect the decision (that took some years), and to embrace a future with hope.

As Mass attendance was dwindling, an infusion of more people would lead to some growth and viability for the long term. Both former parishes were grieving, and the pastoral staff had to be sensitive to it all.

What began as a profound pastoral challenge eventually became an opportunity to become a new and vibrant faith community that continues to become one family of faith today.

We can learn something from that experience; what started out as pain, hurt, confusion, anger, and chaos turned into healing, peace, reconciliation, love, and hope for a brighter future.

When the abuse scandal surfaced in the early 2000s, I chose to remove myself from ministering directly to children and youth in parish programs. The motivating factor was quite simple, really: a male lay leader could easily become a target of a false allegation of abuse considering the climate of that day. I wanted no part of that.

I chose to become certified as a pastoral associate. Since 2004, I have served as one, first in the Manchester, New Hampshire diocese and since 2006 in the Boston archdiocese. The majority of my work is engagement with the adult members of faith communities and in a variety of spiritual, formational, pastoral, and educational opportunities.

CHAPTER 10

The Church Continues to Do Good Works

When the news of 2017 highlighted the abuse cases in the Pennsylvania dioceses, along with the rumors and news regarding questionable behavior of St. John's Seminary in Boston, the Cardinals Wuerl and McCarrick issues, and the growing list of district attorneys across this country investigating our dioceses, the morale of Catholics hit another low—as if we could go lower!

Those news accounts have resurfaced some of that anger and outrage within me once again that has compelled me to come forward—finally—to tell my story. It has also resurfaced the question within me: *Why do I continue to serve the church? Am I part of the problem?*

My love of parish ministry increases every day. Laypersons, religious brothers and sisters, and our priests and deacons are afforded unique opportunities each and every day to engage with people who are at a physical, emotional, and spiritual crossroads in their lives.

We help to bury the dead. We help to celebrate baptisms and weddings, and other sacramental moments—those gateway moments. We listen to a diagnosis of cancer, of heart disease, etc. We help to comfort the afflicted, and occasionally, we are called upon to afflict the comfortable.

We intersect at the hopes and the joys of life alongside the grief, the despair, and the eventual death. Ministry is not for all people, but it is for those of us who are truly called by God to serve God and others in this chaotic world. I was called to engage with that type of ministry.

For the past thirty-five years, I have worked with some amazing priests, heroic priests—men who have taken their vows seriously, men who work in the trenches to promote social justice issues, men who take their call seriously to proclaim the Word not only from the pulpit but also in the streets.

I've worked with gifted men called to priesthood and who are also willing to share the leadership within a faith community with qualified laypeople as "coworkers and coequals in the vineyard." These good men, these good priests are the norm. We need to be doing more to support them! I've also worked side by side with some priests and laypeople too who are egocentric, narcissistic, or, in today's political vernacular, what some might call "Trumpian."

These are the priests who typically destroy parish life and parish growth. They destroy what was done by their predecessors and generally wreak havoc upon parishioners. They don't allow other voices to participate in leadership. How and why they continue as pastors infuriates me frequently, but knowing the numbers available to shepherd our faith communities these days, I fully understand the issues we face as a church. Isn't it time to think outside the box with regard to priesthood and leadership roles in our parishes and diocese?

I believe in the mission of the church as it continues to be stretched and redefined each day. The gap between the "haves" and the "have-nots" widens every day for a variety of reasons, such as poor public policy; creation of laws that destroy the lives of the disenfranchised, the mentally ill, those suffering with addiction issues, the undocumented; and way too many other demographics as well.

The church needs to continue to fill these gaps and be front and center in addressing the needs of all the faithful. As Pope Francis has said many times, the church is in the business of doing triage in the field hospitals of parishes with the broader church serving her people wherever they find themselves in life's journey. Ministry isn't always in the pews. Ministry takes place as we leave Mass to serve the broken, the lonely, the addicted, and the hopeless, bringing light to the darkness.

Perhaps the time has come to have a conversation about the role of parish life coordinators (canon 517.2) that works quite well in other dioceses around the country. Recently, a laywoman was appointed to lead a faith community in Connecticut as a parish life coordinator. Laymen and laywomen and others can pastor a parish. It happens in other parts of the country. The crisis is at hand. Let's reshape the vision.

We are in crisis mode now! Let's continue to pray for vocations to the diocesan priesthood and all other vocations in the church. But let's, at the very least, also have conversations about other models of parish leadership allowing for the shrinking number of the ordained to administer the sacraments, while trained and experienced laity tend to the non-sacramental life of the faith community. It offers us all the hope for vibrant faith communities to continue for the generations to come.

In the summer of 2019, I met with the personnel of the pastoral support and outreach office of the archdiocese. I told my story of abuse. I completed the necessary paperwork to lodge an official complaint against two priests who died long ago.

An assault that took place in 1967 coming to light only now won't really matter to too many people. The religious order of these two priests might at some point reach out to me to offer support, therapy, etc. (to date, they have not). I can meet with other survivors, receive counseling if I choose to, meet with the archbishop, etc., but I continue to move forward, and I remain in the church and in ministry—yet the fatigue factor remains for me.

I've begun to tell trusted individuals of what occurred fifty-plus years ago. The people I've opened up to were shocked, sympathetic, and empathetic. Each time I opened up, it became easier to share. A weight has been lifted.

Telling my story here will only add to the relief, and it may help someone else to share his or her story of abuse. My colleagues have been incredibly supportive.

The question of "Why stay?" still remains, however. Why indeed?

CHAPTER II

A Crisis of Leadership

My personal and ministerial career story is intended to highlight the bigger crisis we have in the church and in our society as well today: it is a crisis of leadership on a variety of levels.

I'm not assigning blame just at the top but rather throughout all of the church's various leadership roles from our pastoral centers and chanceries, right down to the parish level as well.

As a church, we became quite arrogant with our packed churches every Sunday, with an abundance of priests and religious brothers and sisters to staff parishes and schools. We had full seminaries, and our parochial schools had wait-lists. Today, we face a crisis.

We built new churches, and many ethnic parishes were established for the immigrant waves that came to this country: the Irish, Italians, Polish, French, Lithuanians, and many others. Each had their own place to worship. We built Catholic hospitals and nursing and care facilities in major cities around the country. We had it all, and more.

When I speak of the bigger crisis, I'm referring to those individuals—lay and ordained—who lack a bold vision to lead others through crisis. Many of us lead people through crisis every day in our parishes.

Individuals and families know crisis on many levels: loss of a job and an income; the loss of one's good health; the loss of a child, a grandchild, or a spouse; the loss of a parent or a sibling. Institutions, secular and religious, face calamities every day. Bold leaders are required to move away from the crisis and toward a mode of recovery, a mode of reparation and toward stabilization and eventual growth.

How can the Catholic Church today recover from the clergy sex-abuse scandals that continue to haunt and destroy lives today? What can laypeople, clerics, and others from outside the church do together to reshape our leadership, revision our future, reimagine our purpose, and reinspire the people of God?

We can start with intentional and purposeful listening—listening to the real anguish and the profound suffering of the people of God. Don't be tone-deaf. The sins of the past—all of them—need to be brought forward until all the facts have been made public.

The number of abuse cases since the *Charter for the Protection of Children and Young People* (the *Dallas Charter*) has seen a dramatic shift in the claims of clergy abuse. Statistics tell us today that we are finally beginning to address the problems. Pre-2002, we were negligent and complicit on many levels.

Post-2002, we've done a much-better job being transparent about the past, yet we appear to some individuals to be tone-deaf at times about how to serve the victims. We can and must do so much more!

Many of the past sins committed and hidden in the darkness have been brought to light, though we'll continue to hear of more and more dioceses who will be forced to report the sins of the past to local law enforcement authorities. That's a good thing.

We need that full disclosure to move forward. Some bishops—not all—have opened their personnel files and have acknowledged the wrongdoings and the abuse perpetrated by church leadership. It has to be so very frustrating and quite demoralizing for the good priests to hear about their brother priests who harmed others—you've been lumped in with the bad priests!

Until all our bishops make public the records of past abuse regardless of when the abuse took place, this crisis of authentic and purposeful pastoral leadership will haunt us and it will destroy us from within. Recovery won't happen, and we as a church will continue to be more and more irrelevant in a world in need of a moral compass.

Our pews are emptying. Our people are hurting. Our priests are aging. Our ordinations are down. Our morale is low. Collections are dropping. Nights of prayer for reparation are not enough. A rosary for healing is not enough. Benediction for a hurting church is not enough. Bishops fasting is not enough. Ask the victims what is needed!

We don't need an expensive television production featuring the Gregorian chant playing in the background, with an image of a gold tabernacle, candlelit candelabras on an altar, nor glossy publications and a full media campaign to boost the image of the bishops and the church. That approach only targets the 15 percent (more or less) of the Catholics who remain in the pews for now—a lesser percentage now due to COVID-19.

It doesn't speak to the victims who have died, or to the victims who are in still in treatment, or to the victims who have been forced to abandon their faith, or to the victims who remain silent in the church. We need to take our cues from the perspective of the victim.

The intent by clerical leadership at times to repair, to make reparations comes across as an attempt to simply improve the image of the bishops and the church. I am quite certain it is well-intentioned, but much more is needed today, and please let survivors and all the laity participate in this process of reparation and healing. Survivors need to participate in the healing process too. It's why I'm finally speaking out. It will take courage for others to speak out, but it's an emotional risk at the very least.

What we need, what survivors and the church need together, are many more bold voices who will speak up, who will speak out, and who will demand more: more from our priests, more from our bishops and archbishops, more from the USCCB, and much more from Rome—all who have been aware for decades of this crisis.

We need a laity to be well-informed, well-involved, and well-prepared so they might be like those early disciples who had no idea where they were going or what opposition they would be facing, as they brought the authentic message of Christ to hostile crowds.

We need a church hierarchy that is willing to bend toward the laity on the many issues we face together as a church. We are called today through our common baptism to work collaboratively with our priests and bishops. Let the work continue to reshape us all!

CHAPTER 12

From Chaos to Hope

The Catholic Church today continues to come under fire for the sins of the past and the present-day failures in several areas, and rightfully so! We held deep and dark secrets, dark and horrific stories of abuse that should have been revealed in real time as they were occurring.

Whenever that first act of abuse took place, followed by the sin of a cover-up, that was the time to make known, to make public the name of the priest and the members of the hierarchy that protected and concealed this information and the evidence of the crime. That first sin led to countless others.

We had a system that protected the clergy and offending laity as well, those who committed such crimes while protecting these individuals from punishment of any kind. We often relocated priests to other parts of the diocese or other dioceses entirely across the country. Think about that for a moment. We were complicit ruining the lives of countless individuals. It was like a witness protection program for abusers, relocating criminals rather than making them accountable.

Today, at last, we have many safeguards in place to protect our children and our youth, the elderly, and others in our parishes. We require background checks on all volunteers, screening of all staff members, employees, etc.

We require everyone to attend training prior to serving in the church in any capacity. Programs teach of the warning signs of predatory behavior and how children can be groomed, and teaches attendees about best practices to protect children, youth, and the elderly as well. If anyone refuses to go through this training and screening process, they simply don't serve the church in any capacity. We teach age-appropriate curriculum in our faith formation programs, teaching our young people about all aspects of safety as citizens in our world today.

We often go to very extreme and necessary measures to make certain we are never alone with a child in a church setting, never alone in a classroom at the end of a night of teaching children about their faith, never alone in a building with a person seeking some spiritual direction—all to avoid the possibility of having an allegation of abuse. Wish we had thought of this decades ago! It has made some of us times overly cautious and perhaps nervous to engage with people.

How did we get here? What happened? How do we keep fixing it? Who needs to be involved in the repair work? How do we reenergize our people? How do we refocus our purpose and mission in our parishes and in the world today? These questions and many others all involve one important word: LEADERSHIP.

How did we get here? Church leadership failed us on many levels.

What happened? Church leadership covered up what happened.

How do we fix it? Leadership, including new voices and new approaches to leadership, needs to be involved in the decision-making process in parishes, chanceries and pastoral centers, dioceses, and throughout the world in which we serve.

Who needs to be involved? We need more pastoral leaders who will be deeply committed to the purpose and mission of the Catholic Church. We need bold pastoral leaders who will stand up to the power structure within our parishes and dioceses. It all starts locally. Pastoral leaders, both lay and the ordained, working collaboratively are needed today to make our purpose and mission come alive and become relevant again.

Pastoral leaders are needed to be bold and courageous to lead us away from the suffering, away from the pain and the anguish forced upon our brothers and sisters in Christ. We can continue to rise up from this crisis together being a better church in spite of all the hardships caused by some flawed individuals.

Leadership requires each one of us to take critical actions to move our local pastoral needs forward to the people we serve. Our parishes are hemorrhaging. Every new story of a cover-up or a claim of abuse adds to that hemorrhaging.

We need to reverse the issue we all face today of poor morale from the people in the pews and with our pastoral leaders. I don't blame any of us for feeling discouraged. But we need hope. We're in a funk that becomes extremely frustrating at times because of the actions of others. How can we be that face of Christ in the world today when the only thing we hear about is the bad news? We all have good things happening in our faith communities, but they are drowned out by the negativity.

Our seminaries need to prepare and form good and holy men for priesthood in a church in need of such men. Is it time to look at new models of priesthood? Should we look at a married priesthood? Should we be looking at women as deacons? Women as priests? Is the male celibate model of priesthood in need of review and reshaping? Yes to each of these important questions!

How can a vocations office and our parishes approach young men today inviting them to a vocations-awareness night? How do we tell a parent that their son might have a calling? How do we do the work we need to do within this chaos that we didn't create? We need to be people of hope. We need good men. We need holy men, and the time has come for a more prominent place for women!

Our local and universal needs increase every day. Our people, our communities, and our society need pastoral leaders today more than any other time perhaps. Pastoral leadership doesn't always require a particular degree from a prestigious school or university. Ordinary people throughout history have done courageous things in order to lead.

The leadership we need today in the church begins with each one of us as we further develop our own passion for what we do every day. We must recommit ourselves to serving Christ before we can even think about leading others. We need to examine our own flaws and darkness that prevent us at times from being authentic pastoral leaders.

None of us were born leaders. We became, or are still becoming, leaders through the people we serve. When we serve, people embrace us. It is others who make us trusted pastoral leaders, not the degree or a particular certification we might possess.

When we make ourselves better as individuals first, then and only then can we become the pastoral leaders needed in the church, in society, and in the world today. That is hard and necessary work sometimes, but self-improvement—being aware of our limitations, working to improve upon them, and seeking guidance in prayer and in conversations with trusted others—makes us emerge as better individuals and thus better leaders for our faith communities.

Each of us have people who come to us and reveal their lives to us. This is a sacred trust. They trust us with their stories of faith, their hopes and their joys, their tears and their sorrows, and it is that type of intimacy that makes us pastoral leaders.

All the academic degrees and certificates, the variety of ministerial experiences, the requirements needed to be certified in our particular areas of ministry are all well and good and needed, but our ability to listen, to discern, to reflect, to encourage, to support, and to accompany others is what ministry is about.

Our church, our society, our world today are crying out for effective pastoral and decent people to lead. Men with women, lay with the ordained, all who are purpose driven and committed to making a difference are desperately needed.

We need to rise above the falling debris all around us, climbing up to a higher ground in the midst of the chaos. Our people in the pews are looking to us to lead them. Often it is just our presence—that quiet gift of listening—that allows others to place their trust and their very lives in our hands. This is sacred.

We attend a meeting, we meet people coming through the doors of the church, we answer a phone call, and it is that attentive presence more than our words or actions that makes an impression on others. How we show up for the people we serve is a far-better message than what we have to say.

The chaos of life is where we minister often. Deaths, illness, divorce, abuse, poverty, homelessness, loneliness, and other dark places in life are where we meet people. The stakes are high for these people who come to us. Lip service, being tone-deaf to their realities, and not really listening lead to our demise as individuals and as a church. We fail people sometimes. We must stop that! We minister in the midst of disruption at times. The church needs individuals who can and want to embrace these disruptions and work to find a resolve. It is a sacred calling.

We need more pastoral leaders who can thrive and navigate through the raging waters of today. The ability to respond must be part of our skill set; they don't teach it in the seminary, in colleges, etc. You develop it overtime and with the people who come to trust us with their faith journey. Each and every encounter reshapes us.

The low morale we all face at times must be seen as a teachable moment—another gateway moment. We all had to learn about the scandal(s), how to address it with our people, how to help victims, how to train parishioners in the prevention and the reporting of abuse, etc. The safety nets are in place, and we must remain vigilant to protect others and prevent further scandal.

We've all gained insights, we've learned a lot of data about abuse, we've had to overcome obstacles and disappointments in ministry, but we've emerged from this teachable moment as better pastoral leaders—I hope. We've had to address our own emotions and behaviors in this process to become more effective leaders for others.

The experience of crisis has taught us that discernment is essential—patiently listening to God to help sort out our emotions, to sort out what is truth, to sort our own plan of ministerial action that is needed. Discernment helps us to identify WHAT WE CAN DO, WHAT WE CANNOT DO, and WHAT WE WILL NEED to lead others.

I learned years ago that ministry is messy at times, and it can be lonely as well. We can feel fatigued and very isolated from other staff members at times over an issue in the parish. We dig in on how something might be achieved. We think we know best. If we are going to be pastoral leaders, we have to accept the messiness, the fatigue, and the loneliness at times. We don't always need to have answers for others.

We have to stand firm about our convictions while at the same time be a good listener for a colleague who also has convictions and passion. I know I struggle with this issue a great deal.

Today, we seek to be part of the solution to address people's anger, confusion, anxiety, and low morale. We can be paralyzed at times, but we must move on and encounter, engage with the problems at hand, and be braver and more focused than ever before. Our darkest doubts must be voiced, acknowledged, and honored.

We grow in our own faith through this cathartic process. We must always be asking "What's really important in our roles as ministers? What are those pillars that hold us up, that prop up our vision? Can we make an impact as pastoral leaders in our roles in our parishes and in the diocese?" We must contribute to the moral, the intellectual, the emotional, and the spiritual infrastructure that is so desperately needed by our church in these rocky times.

By digging in, we see the need to rebuild. We dig in because of the larger purpose we all serve. We are at center stage, and the curtain is going up in a few minutes. Do we know our lines? Do we know how and where to engage? We reflect, then we respond. We dig into the chaos. We converse *and* we listen.

We remain aware of the suffering, and we offer hope. We dig into the chaos to bring about a healthy and worthy change. We dig in by taking care of ourselves. We read, we reflect, and we pray often. We take some time away. We retreat. We then become better equipped to lead. We become a stronger self when we practice these disciplines.

We dig in by developing our ability to empathize, to really know what is before us from the perspective of the one who is suffering. We become their voice when they cannot speak. We empathize because we share a common mission with those we serve.

As pastoral leaders, we are called to love, to respect, to pay attention to the needs of others, to offer kindness, to use humor, to embrace humility, to be accessible, and to invite others to follow Christ in our world today—when the world is often following something else.

We might well indeed be witnessing low morale and darkness. The darkness has been there before us throughout the decades and centuries, but as we continue to seek out truth, we are called to shed light on the darkness.

We can all be agents of change to move away from the malaise and to make our church relevant again. People with character will lead us. We can ignore and turn away from the noise, OR we can deliberately face the challenges and opportunities before each one of us. It is our sacred obligation to enter into the noise and confusion and chaos at times.

We exist for others. We embody Christ and his concerns for all who suffer. Like Christ, we can inform others. Like Christ, we can form others. And like Christ, we can transform others. We no longer accept the status quo, what was in the past, for that is the inferior approach of pastoral leadership.

We are called to be that creative voice crying out in the wilderness offering creative change. Pastoral leadership is messy, grueling, and can be exhausting at times. Our resolve is to create again and again something good from the crisis of our leadership. We are being called to be reshaped again and again.

We are called to engage with the messiness and remain focused on the mission. The door has been opened to us. I beg that we all go through that door and lead.

CHAPTER 13

Why Do I Remain?

Why indeed? I've heard others explain their reasons. Conferences have been organized on the topic of "Why stay?" both locally and nationally. Books and articles will be published on the topic going forward as well, I'm certain. But they don't answer the question "Why do I remain?"

It begins with my relationship with Christ and my understanding and appreciation of that Eucharistic celebration we can encounter each day or each weekend. It continues each day with a Eucharistic mandate at the end of Mass to go out into the world to spread the Gospel message to others in our homes, neighborhoods, and wherever we might encounter others. It is a sacred calling.

It is through my full and active participation in our liturgical celebrations of Word and sacrament where I most feel the mystique of God's activity in my life. I'm sure it exists in other faith traditions, but the Catholic Church is where I want to continue to live out my baptismal calling.

Prior to his death, Jesuit priest Alfred Delp—hanged in 1945 for his opposition to Adolf Hitler—wrote an essay from his Nazi prison cell about the shaking reality of Advent. As people, we need to be shaken sometimes. We might do everything within our power to fight off being shaken by God, but being shaken can be a gift from God.

Advent and Lent shake and shatter our world as God breaches it again and again. Being shaken and shattered as people and as a church doesn't mean we are to fear these liturgical seasons of wonder and awe. The Spirit is moving about, and he is moving about us and all of reality. The Advent season is about being birthed again and again. Lent brings us into our own passion stories, our own trials and crucifixions, our own deaths, and then our own new lives. Do we see these seasons as same old, same old, OR do we embrace the wonder and awe, ebb and flow of each and every season?

Liturgical seasons help us to restore God's order in our world wherever we can. Wherever God is not known, we are called to make God known. Wherever God is not heard, we are to make God heard. We lend our voice, and so we cocreate with God.

The church and the world need people who have come through crisis emerged and with a new self-awareness and new self-knowledge, even when hounded at times by the residue of pain.

God is shaking humanity right now. The rubble needs to be cleared away. The rebirth of the church awaits our action to make smooth the paths. The relentless models of faith from the Advent story—Mary's "yes" and John's willingness to "cry out"—is all we need to get us started. We must be the type of people who live in wonder and awe of our roles in this church locally and in the world. We owe it to others.

As one survivor said to the bishops, "We need the bishops to make changes to ecclesial policies and the church culture that might ensure that sexual abuse or coercion by anyone in the church, including bishops, is put to an end."

This survivor went on to say, "I ask that you inspire me and our community to be people of faith and hope through your courage and your action, which is needed not in three months, not in six months but right *now*."

CHAPTER 14

Talking and Listening to the People of God: A Possible Road Map for Recovery

There is no single pathway of recovery in life. One must take on and embrace a multitude of approaches to address, fix, and reimagine new ways of being—for organizations, people, for the planet. My pathway of recovery from a sexual assault by members of the clergy was multifaceted, and it had to be!

Society is messed up these days, or has it always been this way? Politics is no longer a noble calling to serve humanity. Priesthood or religious life was once a highly regarded and worthy calling. Organizations and corporations that are profit-driven alone drain every dime from a customer base that cannot get past the need to consume more.

For my organization, the Catholic Church, I believe there is a pathway to recovery that needs to be embraced fifty years ago. We've lost credibility, we've lost people, we've lost revenue, we've lost our moral compass, and we've lost our appeal. So what do we do? How do we begin to move forward? What are the steps we need to take to appear interested to serve others and God again?

We can begin with the anger people feel for us Catholics. Anger is that natural and necessary response to pain, allowing people to vent and express their pain and dismay with us in a nonthreatening manner. Their rage, anger, and other negative feelings about the church is a very reasonable and natural response to be disappointed at the church and her leaders (the pope, bishops, priests, deacons, and lay leaders) and remain upset. Let the anger speak, all of it, then some healing can commence.

Talking and listening to each other help others understand the pain and anger. Avoiding what we feel does not help anyone. We don't need to react, respond, deflect, or try to correct what people are feeling. Correct the misinformation that exists. Continue to have open and honest discussions with the victims and others often. Talking and listening will go a long way in the recovery process, whatever one is recovering from.

Support one another always as pastoral leaders by spending time together in open discussions and in ongoing prayerful experiences for the victims who have died, for the victim survivors, for the church, and for the good priests. There are more good ones than we talk about. Support each other.

Remember, the basic message of the Gospel is not really all that complex as it is about Jesus Christ and our relationship with him individually and collectively. The heart of the Gospel has been distorted by the cover-ups and the predators who have distorted the Gospel of Jesus. Let's fix it! We all have access to the Gospel, not just the ordained or those who feel set apart from the flock. All the baptized have the imprint of God in their hearts and on their lips. Go back to basics.

Do only what you can do, and no more. Live with truthfulness and integrity, putting parishioners and others first and embrace our calling as a church. We often try to do too much to address a crisis yet never listen to what a victim really needs. Listen to the victims of abuse. Keep it simple. Do what they need and *not* what you feel they or we need. Listening is a sacred act!

Teach the truth about our Christian faith. Ensure others always that we, as a church, teach the fullness of our entire faith, especially with regard to sin, forgiveness, justice, grace, morals, and virtue. More than ever before, effective faith formation and a clear proclamation of truths are needed, and those of us who teach and proclaim the truth from the pulpits to the classrooms to the streets must live that truth with complete integrity and transparency each day.

Since we've lost trust in the organization, let's rebuild trust each and every day and with each and every encounter. Trust is built gradually through right relationships. Trust can be shattered in an instant through criminal acts, unkind words and actions, deceit, etc. God's activity in our lives is a slow and lifelong process, and our work with parishioners and others unfolds over the daily interactions through which they come to trust us as parish and diocesan leaders. We have a small window of time to repair and rebuild. Attack the issues now!

Remember all the victims. Remember all those whose lives were damaged by their abusers. Pray constantly for their healing and recovery, and engage with them in a prayer process whenever and as often as possible. Make it a priority. Remember that the church is more than the sum of its parts and more than the actions of its all-too-human members. Remember to pray for and with, when appropriate, the good priests as well. We tend to forget the good priests who have been spiritually damaged as well.

Trust in the slow and steady work of God. We are an impatient people as we want to reach the end without delay and without doing the arduous work. We want to skip over the middle stages, and we grow impatient often. It took decades and centuries to uncover the abuse; it may take decades and centuries to rebuild trust.

We share the pain with all. The pain of the victims and their families is also our pain, and so it is urgent that we reaffirm our commitment to ensure the protection of minors and of vulnerable adults. The wounds will never disappear, and they require us to forcefully condemn the many atrocities. Too often we compartmentalize the pain as having occurred to "others" and not to all of us. When one member suffers, we all suffer.

We must continue to acknowledge as an ecclesial community that we were not where we should have been, that we did not act in a timely manner, realizing the magnitude and the gravity of the damage done to so many lives. Had we responded to the first hints of the atrocities, we may have ended up in a different place. Burying facts, hiding evidence, and relocating priests, bishops, and religious men and women only added to the anger, hatred, mistrust, etc. The acknowledgments must go on for years to come, unfortunately.

Prayer, fasting, and penance—not as token gestures—can help, but more must be done to include victim survivors in all recovery efforts. This can awaken our collective conscience and arouse our solidarity and commitment to a culture of care that says "Never again" to every form of abuse. Let's have the voices and experiences of victims shape our prayer efforts, shape what we fast from, and be the benefactors of the penance they must be rendered.

Never minimize past sins. Whenever we have tried to replace, silence, ignore, or reduce the people of God to smallness, we end up creating communities, projects, theological approaches, spiritualities, and structures without deep roots, without memory, without faces, without bodies, and, ultimately, without lives. The sins remain fresh and raw for many. Do not say we've done so much to see that this shall never happen again. You are simply trying to convince yourself that all's well that ends well. Nothing could be further from the truth. All is not well, and if we minimize the problem, we become 100 percent irrelevant to the world soon.

Clericalism nullifies the character of Christians as it diminishes and undervalues the baptismal graces that the Holy Spirit has placed in the heart of our people. We need our clerics, but we need our laity as well in harmony with the other. These are equal roles with distinct characteristics that are lived out in parishes and in all society. Let's find ways to see complementary roles that are not in competition but rather seen as collegial partners. This is a sacred calling.

Full and active participation of and by all of the church's membership, lay and clerics alike, working to uproot the culture of abuse in all its forms and in all our communities will be successful in generating the necessary dynamics for sound and realistic change. We can no longer have an ill-informed laity passively sitting in pews on Sundays. We all must be aware of our communities' needs: its strengths, weaknesses, opportunities, and threats from within and outside of the parish.

We must return to and recover the original freshness and spirit of the Gospel of Jesus. New avenues can arise, and new paths of creativity will open up with different forms of expression, more eloquent signs and words with new meaning for today's world. We need new voices to shed light upon the Word and its meaning for us today. The words of Scripture never lose relevance unless we stop trying to comprehend their meaning each day. Every day brings us a gospel challenge. Use the Word to grow in understanding of life and of the Word itself.

Collectively, we must further acknowledge and continue to condemn as a church, with sorrow and shame, all the atrocities perpetrated by consecrated persons, clerics, and all those entrusted with the mission of watching over and caring for those most vulnerable, including lay leaders—it wasn't just priests! We have made strides to acknowledge and condemn the sin, but we've only just begun. As a nation, the sin of slavery should always remain fresh in our citizenry's psyche. The same must be said of clergy sex abuse. Recall the victims!

We must beg forgiveness for our own sins and for the sins of others. Popes, bishops, priests, deacons, religious, and laity alike must continue to seek forgiveness as they are representatives of the church. The awareness of the sins helps us to acknowledge our errors, our offenses, our crimes, and the wounds we've caused in the past and allows us, in the present, to be more open and committed along a journey of renewed conversion.

CHAPTER 15

Are We Born to Lead, or Are We Formed to Lead—or Both?

How did I end up where I ended up in life? I'm not, by any means, done being formed. I seek reshaping often in my remaining decades of life. I've another few left in me, I hope, so there's more to "do" and "be" as I approach the retirement phase of life.

Are we born to lead? Not me! I entered life, and I just followed the rules of the house: keep quiet, keep your head down, do what you're told, or I'll give you something to cry about! We followed those rules rather than face wrath. I followed and learned to avoid getting in trouble too often—maybe that was leadership? You decide. I was merely trying to avoid a beating!

Are we formed for leadership? I'd say for me that I reached a phase in life when I wanted to lead others. Because I knew best? Some of that is true. Because my way was the only way? Some of this is true as well! Because in time and through self-transformation, both educationally and physically, I had gained insights—wisdom, perhaps—to see myself as a leader. I embrace that daily, sometimes quietly and other times more boldly.

Every successive parish where I served, every successive semester I taught, every successive retreat I led, every successive talk and presentation I offered to the people of God gave me more and more confidence—something I never thought I lacked. Each encounter has left me with the feeling of "I got this!"

Are we born to lead, or are we formed to lead in time? It's both! I took my time to find my place in the world. I was educated as a child, and nothing I learned appealed to me in any way, shape, or form. After high school, I worked at several jobs—or I showed up. Can't say I really worked during those early jobs.

It was that simple initial invitation to serve that ignited in me some spark for connectivity with others. A simple invite to engage with others led me to putting a bunch of letters and words on these pages, producing a memoir, a story that began in childhood loneliness, grew into an abusive encounter, morphed into moving forward, motivated to not allow a painful encounter shape my identity or future and professionally is wrapping up a thirty-five-plus-year career.

Leaders are born and grow in their leadership throughout life. We're all leaders at birth, perhaps. Some of us need to determine at some point in life how and where to lead.

CONCLUSION

I've heard it for decades that I should write a book. Who on God's created planet would read anything that I put on the pages of a book? Everyone who writes must feel the same way. What could I possibly say in a book that is "book worthy?" I'm still asking that question.

Perhaps this was merely an effort to purge the past from my mind. Well, that didn't happen. Maybe a book would make me rich and famous. I'm rich beyond monetary wealth, and fame is not anything I seek. Or more appropriately, I want other victims to know that abuse is never okay and we must reveal it, expose it, and purge it from society in all its forms.

The abuse never defined me; I didn't allow it. The abuse didn't discourage me from a vocation in the Catholic Church. If anything, I dug in deeper to serve the church in a variety of ways for three-plus decades. I've used the abuse to be more vigilant of policies to protect not only children and adolescents but also the elderly. All forms of abuse can never be tolerated in churches, organizations, and society as a whole. It must be exposed each and every time!

So these pages you've read have told you one man's story—one man's journey of faith, of self-discovery, and of transformation. There's nothing heroic in my story. Had there been some heroics, the story might have been more interesting for you, the reader!

Every one of us has the ability to tell our stories in print, in other media formats, in blogs and in podcasts, or even by keeping a private journal. Whatever format we choose to tell our tales, we just need to do it! Our experiences can aid others in their recovery. Our recovery and reshaping our paths can embolden others to do the same.

I'm not unique. I'm not an author, but I do have a story to be told, and I guess you've just finished reading it.

Your thoughts I welcome!

About the Author

Thomas J. Griffin has been serving Roman Catholic parishes for more than three decades in a variety of roles. Each experience has reshaped him into being a better lay minister. He has been humbled beyond words by the willingness of parishioners and others to share their faith journey with him.

From a simple desire to serve in some leadership capacity in an organization came a career filled with accompanying others in faith. This book has been in the works for years, and only recently has he felt the desire to get it published for other victims, church leaders, and others in leadership roles in all organizations who are called to protect children, adolescents, the elderly, and all other demographics who are vulnerable within our common society. May his effort help at least one person move forward in life.